Bringing
the **NEWS**

EXTRA EXTRA

Bringing *the* NEWS

Joe Grimm

ISBN-13: 978-0-9758-9791-1
ISBN-10: 0-9758-9791-8

(Cover: From advertising poster by Calvert Lithographic Co.,
Detroit, circa 1894)

FOREWORD

PEOPLE HAVE ALWAYS CRAVED THE LATEST NEWS, whether it was delivered from distant places by mail carriers or peddled on street corners by newspaper hawkers. This collection of newsies on postcards shuffles together *The Daily Mail* and the daily mail.

These century-old postcards celebrate newsies in photographs and artwork, in groups or singly, black and white or color. The newsboys—and girls, as well as a few adults—are almost always portrayed in hard-knock ways. Feet and calves are sometimes bare. Patches cling to elbows and knees. They cover their heads with stocking caps or the floppy hats we still know as "newsboys." In romanticized cartoon images and photographs, smiles belie and deny the child labor and exploitation they endured.

With postcards, stamps, and newspapers costing just a penny or two apiece, these were affordable ways to get or send the news.

Adult contractors have replaced newsies, just as e-mail and the Internet are replacing postcards and newspapers. But if there is inside you a scrappy, survive-by-your-wits newsie, you'll enjoy this collection of cards and carriers bringing news in old-fashioned ways.

Acknowledgments

Many thanks to Loren Ghiglione, former dean of Northwestern University's Medill School of Journalism; Neal Shine, late publisher of the *Detroit Free Press;* Pete Waldmeir, former columnist at *The Detroit News,* and John Bentley, longtime circulation executive at the Detroit Media Partnership. Thanks also to Alex Cruden of the *Detroit Free Press* and Marsha Low, formerly of the *Free Press,* for editing, and to Maya Rhodes of Wayne State University Press for her design work.

"Extra"

Long before adult independent contractors, motor routes, and home delivery, "newsies" were critical to a newspaper's success. Most newspapers were sold within the cities where they were published. Boys and some girls would purchase copies at the newspaper office and rush out to the street corners to "hustle sheets." Armies of competing newsies became foot soldiers in circulation wars. Fighting for territory and shouting out titillating headlines, this sales force helped put food on immigrant and poor families' tables.

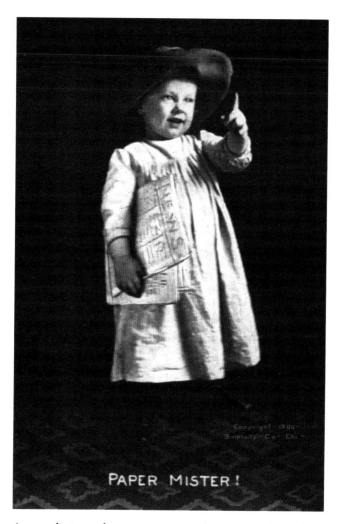

PAPER MISTER!

A tantalizing tale meant money in a newsie's pocket. Soft stories meant slow sales and slack stomachs. Newsies got creative: "Twenty-two people swindled!" shouted a newsboy. It was enough to make a man dig up the coins in his pocket for a copy. Moving along a half block later, the boy improved his pitch: "Twenty-*three* people swindled!" This tale was told by Bill Blackbeard, founder and curator of the San Francisco Academy of Comic Art, to Loren Ghiglione, who was working on *The American Journalist: Paradox of the Press.*

Mark Twain was a newspaper writer who lionized the newsies who sold his work. In *A Connecticut Yankee in King Arthur's Court* he wrote, ". . . outside there rang clear as a clarion a note that enchanted my soul and tumbled thirteen worthless centuries about my ears: 'Camelot WEEKLY HOSANNAH AND LITERARY VOLCANO!—latest irruption—only two cents—all about the big miracle in the Valley of Holiness!' One greater than kings had arrived—the newsboy."

Not all newsies were boys. An 1881 *Harper's Weekly* cartoon recounted the girls' joy at an excursion from which they were excluded—leaving them to hawk as many papers as they could carry that day, and pockets full of coins to take home that night.

"There are 10,000 children living on the streets of New York. . . . The newsboys constitute an important division of this army of homeless children. You see them everywhere. . . . They rend the air and deafen you with their shrill cries. They surround you on the sidewalk and almost force you to buy their papers. They are ragged and dirty. Some have no coats, no shoes, and no hat."

— James B. McCabe, Jr., writer, 1872

Poor little newsboy, sad your lot!
Cold, hungry, homeless you.
Think not that you are all forgot,
Brave hearts are tender, too!

As head of the Children's Aid Society, Charles Loring Brace helped New York City's neglected street children in the mid and late 1800s. Many were homeless newsies, so he helped build newsboy lodging houses. Other cities did, too. Brace also organized classes, camps, and "Orphan Trains" which, over 75 years, moved 200,000 neglected children from New York City to families in the Midwest where they were raised and sometimes adopted. Some call Brace the father of modern foster care.

"I remember one cold night seeing some ten or a dozen of the little homeless creatures piled together to keep each other warm beneath the stairway of the (New York) *Sun* office. There used to be a mass of them also at *The Atlas* office, sleeping in the lobbies, until the printers drove them away by pouring water on them. One winter, an old burnt-out safe lay all the season in Wall Street, which was used as a bedroom by two boys who managed to crawl into the hole that had been burned."

—*Charles Loring Brace, 1866*

New Year's Greetings to ye Future

In New York City, newsboys went on strike in July, 1899, over a ten-cent increase in the charge for one hundred newspapers, from fifty cents to sixty cents. They were not allowed to return unsold papers. *The New York Evening World* and the *New York Evening Journal* had raised the price when the Spanish-American War drove up newspaper sales. They would not reduce it after the war ended and sales slackened. The newsies said that they were left with little or no profit. A leader of the strike, one-eyed "Kid Blink," said: "Ten cents on the dollar is as much to us as it is to Mr. Hearst, the millionaire. Am I right, boys? We can do more with ten cents than he can do with twenty-five." The strike ended in August with the publishers keeping the new price, but allowing the newsies to return unsold papers for full refunds.

Kid Blink Beats the World, by Don Brown, tells the story of the one-eyed newsboy who led the 1899 New York strike against the newspapers. The illustrated book, published in 2004, is aimed at young readers.

THEY GET OUT AN "EXTRA" HERE EVERY TIME I SAY ANYTHING. "ISHKABIBLE!"

In 1992, The Walt Disney Co. gambled on a movie musical with "Newsies," the story of the 1899 newsboys' strike. Box office sales were disappointing, but it has achieved cult status on the Internet. Fan sites and trading posts have given "Newsies" new life.

Papers is all I got
Wish I could catch a breeze
Sure hope the headline's hot
All I can catch is fleas
God help me if it's not
Somebody help me, please.

If I hate the headline, I'll make up the headline
And I'll say anything I hafta
'Cause it's two for a penny, if I take too many
Weasel just makes me eat 'em afta.

           —From the Disney movie musical "Newsies"

On the Road to The Great Serpent Mound.
Locust Grove near Peebles, Ohio.

The National Child Labor Committee worked to end child exploitation with tougher state and federal laws. A teacher-turned-photographer/investigator, Lewis Hine gave the effort some of its most powerful arguments. He criss-crossed the country, photographing the plight of newsies, as well as children working in factories and fields.

Adams Street, looking North, Peoria, Ill.

As a pre-teen, Thomas A. Edison hawked candy and newspapers aboard the Grand Trunk Railroad on its daily run from his home in Port Huron, Michigan, to Detroit. Showing his inventive ways, he founded his own *Grand Trunk Herald,* likely the first newspaper published on a train.

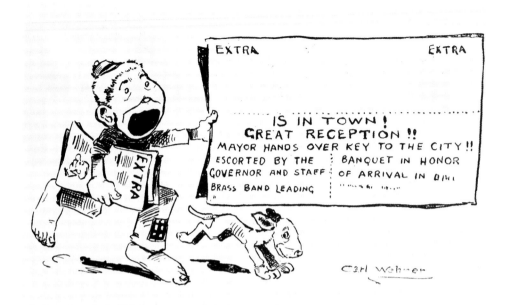

Horatio Alger, Jr., championed the scrappy American spirit in more than a hundred dime novels published in the late nineteenth century. Some of his street heroes were featured in *Life Among the New York Newsboys* (1869), *The Chicago Newsboy* (1889), and *Nelson the Newsboy* (1901). The newsletter of the Horatio Alger Society is "The Newsboy."

Around the turn of the twentieth century, parlor songs and dances romanticized fleet-footed newsies with "The Newsboy's Story," "The Newsboy Gallop," "Newsboy Polka," and "Newsboy Schottische."

EXTRA! EXTRA!!
MERRY CHRISTMAS

Later, it was movies. Some were: "The Newsboy" (1895), "A Newsboy's Scrap" (1897), "The Newsy and the Tramp" (1911), "A Newsboy's Luck" (1911), "The Newsboy's Debt" (1914), "The Newsboys' Home" (1938), and "King of the Newsboys" (1938).

The "Newsboy Cap," soft, rounded and flat with a small bill, has had many names. They include the descriptive "Button Top" as well as "Touring Cap," "Longshoreman's Hat," "Fisherman's Cap," "Lundberg Stetson," "Gatsby," and "Big Apple." They have been called Dai caps in Wales, Cheese-cutters in New Zealand and Canada and a Sixpence in Norway. Newsboys have been made of wool, leather, suede, tweed, and vinyl. They have been in and out of fashion for about five hundred years.

I'm extra fond of you

Newsboys have risen to high places. When Sir Wilfred Laurier, the Canadian prime minister in 1896-1911, traveled out west from the capital city of Ottawa, he stepped off the train, bought a newspaper and had a long conversation about politics and personal aspirations with the boy who had sold it to him. The boy, John Diefenbaker, reportedly ended the conversation with, "Well, Sir Wilfrid, I can't waste any more time; I have to sell my papers." Laurier quoted the lad's remarks in a speech that evening. And, in 1957, that newsie became prime minister of Canada, too.

St. Paul Dispatch [EXTRA]

... IS IN TOWN !
GREAT RECEPTION !!
MAYOR HANDS OVER KEY TO THE CITY !!
BANQUET IN HONOR | ESCORTED BY THE
OF ARRIVAL IN ... | GOVERNOR AND STAFF !
BRASS BAND LEADING !

THEY GOT OUT AN **EXTRA** FOR ME.

COPYRIGHT 1906 BY A.T. MALONEY, DENVER POST

In 1952, the United States issued a commemorative postage stamp to recognize the people who connected newspaper publishers and readers. The green three-center shows a carrier whose bag bears the slogan, "Busy Boys . . . Better Boys." The stamp paid tribute to "Free Enterprise" and "the important service rendered to their communities and their Nation."

In 1982, the Postal Service marked the 150th anniversary of Horatio Alger's birth, printing a stamp with four boys, one of them holding a newspaper aloft.

Sometimes, a newsboy makes headlines. One such occasion came in November 1871, when the three-masted sailing bark named *Newsboy* collided with the *E.B. Allen*, bound from Chicago for Buffalo with a hold full of grain. The *Allen* sank south of Thunder Bay Island in Lake Huron and the *Newsboy* continued on into the fog.

In the late 1800s, drug stores and tobacconists gave away black-and-white or sepia photographs with the sale of Newsboy brand plug chewing tobacco. Printed on four by six cardstock, the images were called "cabinets" because they were to be displayed in cabinets where they would be protected. The cards featured actors, celebrities, and landscapes.

As everyone knows, Superman is the alter-ego of mild-mannered *Daily Planet* reporter Clark Kent. Less well known is that comic-book hero Captain Marvel is the alter-ego of homeless newsboy Billy Batson. The newsboy received his powers from the wizard Shazam after he followed a stranger into an abandoned subway tunnel. In 1941, Captain Marvel rescued another orphaned newsboy, Freddy Freeman, from the evil Captain Nazi and gave him powers, too, changing him into Captain Marvel, Jr.

Newsboy bands formed in several cities, including Los Angeles, Toledo, Cincinnati, Sioux City, Edmonton, and Grand Rapids, Michigan. Chicago had at least two, one organized by the *Chicago Daily News,* another by the *Chicago Defender. Defender* drummer Lionel Hampton grew up to be a jazz legend.

AN EXTRA   MERRY
              CHRISTMAS

That's what
I'm wishing
you.

In the weeks before Christmas, adults across the country donate their time to the Goodfellows or Old Newsboys, groups that sell special-edition newspapers to help buy gifts for poor children. In Detroit, inspiration for such an effort came from a cartoon in *The Detroit News.* The Burt Thomas drawing showed a well-dressed man delivering Christmas to a poor family. At the urging of some caring Detroiters, the Detroit Newsboy Association joined the effort, working under the motto: "No kiddie without a Christmas." The group has raised millions to provide toys, clothes, dental care, and camp scholarships.